I BELIEVE

It Is Easy to Be Kind and Good to One Another and to Animals, Just Like Baxter, the Magnificent Dog

Coloring and Activity Book 6

SUZANNE MONDOUX
Illustrated by Gaëtanne Mondoux

BALBOA PRESS
A DIVISION OF HAY HOUSE

Balboa Press books may be ordered through booksellers or by contacting:

Balboa Press
A Division of Hay House
1663 Liberty Drive
Bloomington, IN 47403
www.balboapress.com
1 (877) 407-4847

Because of the dynamic nature of the Internet, any web addresses or links contained in this book may have changed since publication and may no longer be valid. The views expressed in this work are solely those of the author and do not necessarily reflect the views of the publisher, and the publisher hereby disclaims any responsibility for them.

The author of this book does not dispense medical advice or prescribe the use of any technique as a form of treatment for physical, emotional, or medical problems without the advice of a physician, either directly or indirectly. The intent of the author is only to offer information of a general nature to help you in your quest for emotional and spiritual well-being. In the event you use any of the information in this book for yourself, which is your constitutional right, the author and the publisher assume no responsibility for your actions.

Any people depicted in stock imagery provided by Getty Images are models, and such images are being used for illustrative purposes only. Certain stock imagery © Getty Images.

Print information available on the last page.

ISBN: 978-1-9822-2268-0 (sc)
ISBN: 978-1-9822-2281-9 (e)

Balboa Press rev. date: 02/22/2019

This book belongs to

_____

I am _____ years old

One beautiful winter afternoon happy Baxter, a black and white Pointer Mix, was playing chase in a field with other dogs and people friends. Big white snowflakes fell from the sky. He bounced in and out of the fluffy snow.

Baxter had many friends and loved to play with everyone. But he was a bit nervous around dogs that were smaller than him.

Later that afternoon Carlo and Teddy came running through the snowy field. Baxter had never met these two horses before. He had seen many horses but not in this field.

Baxter was excited and happy to see new animals. He would have new friends to play with. With as much might as he could muster he leaped in and out of the snow as fast as he could towards Carlo and Teddy.

Suddenly, Baxter stopped in his tracks and stood on top of the snow. His legs sunk slowly beneath the snow. He pawed his way back out of the snow and crawled on his belly towards the horses.

The snow was a bit less soft where Carlo and Teddy were standing. Baxter stood back up on his four feet. He glared at the little fawn colored Pug dog standing in between Teddy and Carlo.

Pug's little curly tail waged with excitement. She was so happy to see Baxter. She ran right up to him. Baxter backed away. He was not happy any more. It was a mystery to him why he was not comfortable around dogs that were smaller than him.

Baxter looked up at Carlo and Teddy. "Hello, my name is Baxter."

Carlo and Teddy smiled a big hello and introduced themselves. "We have come from the valley. Our last few days were spent at the ranch with Jojo. Do you know where that is?"

Pug was still wagging her tail waiting for Baxter to pay attention to her. But Baxter would not look at her. With her head down she walked back to Carlo and Teddy.

"Yes, it is just down the mountain over there. You have come a long way up the mountain." Baxter smiled up at Carlo and Teddy. "We don't get many visitors that venture all the way up here."

"We are explorers and decided to follow the trail that led to this place. On our map it is called Baxter the Magnificent playground. This plateau overlooking the meadows is quite impressive with the glitter of white snow and crystal blue streams flowing down the mountain. It must be just as majestic in the spring, summer and autumn."

"Yes, we have a beautiful playground here," said Baxter. He sat in the snow. His smile slowly returned on his face.

"We have brought our friend Lulu to join us. In our pouch are two of her puppies, Bessie and Tulip." Carlo arched his neck back and reached for the pouch dangling from his back. He slowly pulled out the puppies one at a time. Bessie and Tulip bounced in the snow.

Baxter had never seen dogs this small before. He glared down at them. He watched as they jumped and played in and around Carlo and Teddy's feet. Then the puppies ran towards Baxter. They played in and around his legs and pulled and tugged on his tail.

Baxter was very nervous and he stood frozen. He did not know how to be with puppies. Lulu called her pups back to her. The pups ran across the fluffy snow and sunk down beneath the snow. They disappeared before their eyes.

Baxter ran to where the pups had sunk in the snow. He quickly dug beneath the snow. Big brown eyes and two big smiles stared back up at him. He lowered his head and with his teeth he pulled the pups out one at a time from beneath the snow.

Lulu ran to them. Bessie and Tulip were yelping with joy and ran back to Carlo and Teddy where they did not sink in the snow. Before Baxter could step away from her again Lulu gave him a big hug. "Thank you for saving my pups!"

Bessie

Tulip

Baxter's smile grew even bigger. He then remembered why he was not comfortable around dogs that were smaller than him.

He walked with Lulu to where Carlo and Teddy were keeping an eye out on the pups.

"I would like to apologize to Lulu," said Baxter.

"Apologize for what?" asked Teddy.

"For as long as I can remember I did not feel comfortable around dogs that were smaller than me. As a result I was also not very kind to them, or good with them," said Baxter.

"You were very brave today," said Teddy. "You helped Bessie and Tulip from a dangerous situation."

"I was always a happy dog with a big smile. I played a lot and with everyone. But I had never been around other puppies. One day a puppy came to the playground. He was so happy to be here. He ran everywhere and jumped up and down on everything. Then he got hurt." Baxter lowered his head. "It was my fault."

Carlo, Teddy, and Lulu gave Baxter a hug. "Continue with your story," said Lulu.

"Tiny, that was his name. He was a Chihuahua. I stepped on him. He cried so loud and ran to the human he had come to the playground with. Her name was Lucie. She was twelve years old. Tiny was just four months old.

Lucie cried so much because Tiny was crying. She picked Tiny up in her arms and left the playground. They did not return for a long time. But they came back just the other day. Tiny and Lucie wanted to play with me but I felt so bad I could not play with them. Tiny walked away crying again. I did not want to play with him because I was afraid I would hurt him again."

Carlo lowered his head to get closer to Baxter. He wiped the tears from Baxter's eyes. "Baxter, can I make a suggestion. I think it may help you. From what I understand and what I read about you on the map is that you are a very Happy dog. You are a dog that smiles all the time. You are kind and good to everyone that comes to your park. You are kind and good because you know of no other way to be. When you stepped on Tiny you did not mean for that to happen. It was an accident, was it not?"

"Yes. I did not mean to step on him or hurt him," said Baxter looking up at Carlo.

"Even though it was an accident why don't you go to Tiny and apologize?" Carlo nudged Baxter closer to the pups. "Apologize for stepping on him and hurting him. Tell him what you told us. I am sure Tiny and Lucie will understand. Being kind and good sometimes requires saying you are sorry even when it is an accident. I would even say it is just as important to say you are sorry when it is an accident. And being kind and good is also helping another animal or person to feel comfortable and at ease with you, and letting them know that you can be trusted and have a friendship with them."

Baxter sat for a moment in silence. Then he looked up at Carlo. "Are you saying that even though it was an accident I am still responsible for what I did? And because I am responsible for what I did I should apologize and offer my help to make the situation better, offer to do and help in any way I can?"

"You understand very well," said Carlo.

Baxter smiled ear to ear. The way he always smiled.

"I will go over where Tiny and Lucie are playing. Then I will come back and introduce you all to them and the others in the playground," said Baxter.

"We will wait for you, Baxter," said Lulu.

Baxter bounced in and out of the fluffy snow to where Tiny and Lucie were playing.

From that day on Baxter never shied away from anything he did that hurt or made someone cry. With each day he had come to understand what it meant to be kind and good, and how being responsible for his actions, no matter if it was an accident, that his kind and good nature helped him be responsible for everything he said and did.

Over the years everyone came to know of Happy Baxter the Magnificent for being a kind and good dog. He became a legend of kindness and goodness. Baxter welcomed all animals big and small, even much smaller than him to the playground. It was the best playground in the world!

For the next thirty (30) days, Baxter invites you to write one thing you have said or done that you know has hurt or made a person or an animal cry. It can be something you did not mean to do – like an accident, just like Baxter.

Or, it can be something you meant to say or do that hurt or made someone or an animal cry.

Once a day write

1. What you said or did.

2. How you were responsible for saying or doing this.

3. What you will say and do to show you accept responsibility.

4. What you will say and do to correct / make right --- show your kindness and true goodness you have inside you.

5. The outcome, how the other person or animal responded to you for taking responsibility for what you said and did.

6. What you would do differently next time you are in the same situation again where you want to say or do something that will hurt or make someone or an animal cry but you decided to do and say something that is good and kind instead.

7. How do you feel when you do and say the good and kind things that make a person or animal smile and laugh and feel good?

Lets begin.

Most importantly - Have fun!

Remember to smile.

Remember to laugh.

Remember to be curious and ask questions.

Remember to Believe in yourself.

Say out loud 10 times.

I Believe in myself.
I Believe in myself.
I Believe in myself.
I Believe in myself.
I Believe in myself.
I Believe in myself.
I Believe in myself.
I Believe in myself.
I Believe in myself.
I Believe in myself.

Day 1

_____

_____

_____

_____

_____

_____

_____

_____

_____

_____

_____

_____

Day 2

_____

_____

_____

_____

_____

_____

_____

_____

_____

_____

_____

_____

Day 3

_____

_____

_____

_____

_____

_____

_____

_____

_____

_____

_____

_____

_____

_____

Day 4

Day 5

Day 6

Day 7

_____

_____

_____

_____

_____

_____

_____

_____

_____

_____

_____

_____

Day 8

Day 9

Day 10

_____

_____

_____

_____

_____

_____

_____

_____

_____

_____

_____

Day 11

_____

_____

_____

_____

_____

_____

_____

_____

_____

_____

_____

_____

_____

Day 12

Day 13

_____

_____

_____

_____

_____

_____

_____

_____

_____

_____

_____

_____

Day 14

_____

_____

_____

_____

_____

_____

_____

_____

_____

_____

_____

_____

Day 15

_____

_____

_____

_____

_____

_____

_____

_____

_____

_____

_____

_____

Day 16

Day 17

Day 18

Day 19

Day 20

_____

_____

_____

_____

_____

_____

_____

_____

_____

_____

_____

_____

Day 21

_____

_____

_____

_____

_____

_____

_____

_____

_____

_____

_____

_____

_____

Day 22

Day 23

Day 24

Day 25

Day 26

_____

_____

_____

_____

_____

_____

_____

_____

_____

_____

_____

Day 27

Day 28

Day 29

_____

_____

_____

_____

_____

_____

_____

_____

_____

_____

_____

_____

Day 30

WOW! YOU ARE AMAZING!!!!!!!!!!!!!!

YOU DID ALL THE FUN STUFF!

YOU PARTICIPATED IN 30 DAYS OF FUN!

KEEP GOING!

EXPLORE YOUR IMAGINATION!

BELIEVE IN YOURSELF ALWAYS!

SHARE WHAT YOU WROTE AND THE EXPLORATION
OF YOUR IMAGINATION WITH A FRIEND!

THANK YOU FOR BEING GOOD AND
KIND TO EVERY ANIMAL.

On behalf of all the ANIMALS – thank you for
making this a better world for ALL OF US!